ONCE UPON A TOM
BY
ANTHONY QUINN PAYNE

THIS IS FOR ALL OF OUR CHILDREN
TO BUILD BRIGHTER AND CLEANER FUTURES.
IT TOUCHES MY HEART WHEN CHILDREN FOLLOW US.

ISBN: 1514270595
ISBN 13: 9781514270592

Once upon a time, there was a boy named Tom, who lived in a town that wasn't so fond.

Filled with pollution, Tom always looked for solutions to clean up his town and offer green substitutions.

Sell your books at
sellbackyourBook.com!

Go to sellbackyourBook.com
and get an instant price quote.
We even pay the shipping - see
what your old books are worth
today!

00003252529241

VG

9241

0003252

As Tom walked through his town, he found garbage on the ground and smog so thick it was hard to breathe around.

Industrial waste dumping affected the waters,
harming all the creatures—from birds to otters,
and even humans, too. Drinking unclean water
would leave anyone feeling blue.

Tom picked up the can
the man dropped from his hand.
"You can recycle this and help save our land!"

The man kept walking as Tom kept talking.
"Sir, pollution is wrong and affects us often."

The man said, "Listen, kid, I don't really care.
It's not affecting me, I'm breathing really clear."

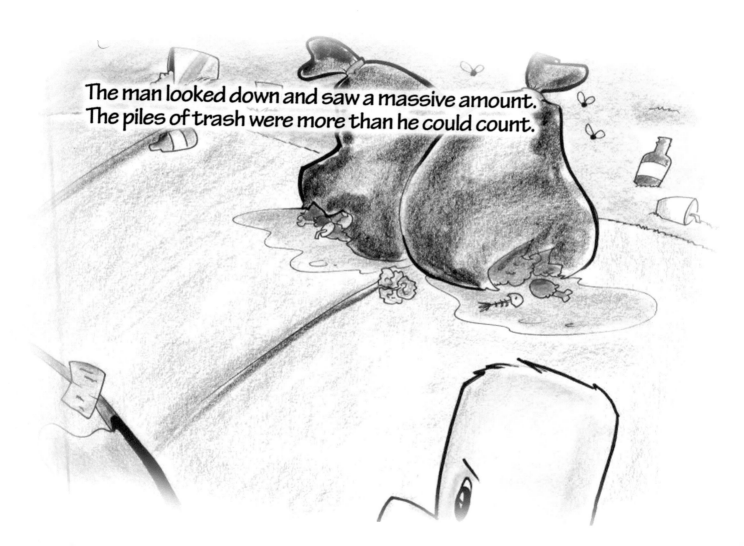

The trees looked sad
with the land so bad,
and the creeks looked more like floating trash pads.
Tom said, "This is hurting our community and not helping our unity!"

The man said, "Wow, kid, you sure know a lot
about neighborhood pollution and our community blocks!"

"Yes, sir!" Tom said. "We have to change our ways,
so we can have greener days,
healthy air, and clean landfills.
A cleaner environment also helps lower your bills.

The man was impressed
with all the knowledge Tom possessed.

As they both kept walking,
the man kept talking
while picking up trash
from paper to plastic to cans and glass.

Words to Discuss:
Recycle
Pollution
Industrial waste
Immense
Contamination
Gruesome
Nuisance
Revolution

Made in the USA
Charleston, SC
04 November 2015